Volume copyright © 1994 by Breslich and Foss
Illustrations © 1997 by Dinah Dryhurst 1994

Published by Silver Dolphin Books
5880 Oberlin Drive, Suite 400
San Diego, CA 92121-9653

Quotations at the beginning of each month are from
Black Beauty by Anna Sewell, originally published in 1877.

Designed by Nigel Partridge

Many of Dinah Dryhurst's illustrations originally
appeared in *Black Beauty*, published in 1993 by Breslich & Foss Ltd.
The remainder are original to this work.

ISBN 1-57145-106-4

Conceived and produced by Breslich & Foss Ltd, London

Printed and bound in Hong Kong

My Best Day

JANUARY

Best Parties and Entertainment

January

My Worst Day

January

My Finest Adventure

FEBRUARY

The air was frosty, the moon bright, and it was very pleasant. We went through a village, through a dark wood, then uphill, then downhill, till after an eight miles' run we came to the town. On through the streets we went and into the Market Place. All was quite still except for the clatter of my feet on the stones – everybody was asleep.

THOUGHTS FOR
FEBRUARY

My Best Day

FEBRUARY

Best Parties and Entertainment

February

My Worst Day

February

My Finest Adventure

MARCH

He hung my rein on one of the iron spikes, and was soon hidden amongst the trees. By the side of the road, a few paces off, Lizzie was standing quietly with her back to me. My young mistress was sitting easily with a loose rein, humming a little song.

THOUGHTS FOR
MARCH

My Best Day

MARCH

Best Parties and Entertainment

MARCH

My Worst Day

_____

_____

_____

_____

_____

_____

_____

_____

_____

_____

_____

_____

MARCH

My Finest Adventure

My Worst Day

APRIL

My Finest Adventure

MAY

One day during this summer the groom cleaned and dressed me with such extraordinary care that I thought some new change must be at hand. He trimmed my fetlocks and legs, passed the tarbrush over my hoofs, and even parted my forelock. I think the harness also had an extra polish.

THOUGHTS FOR
MAY

My Best Day

MAY

Best Parties and Entertainment

MAY

My Worst Day

MAY

My Finest Adventure

_____

_____

_____

_____

_____

_____

_____

_____

_____

_____

_____

_____

JUNE

He led me into my box, took off
the saddle and bridle with his own hands, and tied me up. Calling for
a pail of warm water and a sponge, he took off his coat, and while the
stable man held the pail, he sponged my sides for some time so
tenderly that I was sure he knew how sore and bruised they were.
'Whoa! my pretty one,' he said; 'stand still.' His very voice did me good,
and the bathing was very comforting.

THOUGHTS FOR
JUNE

My Best Day

_____

_____

_____

_____

_____

_____

_____

_____

_____

_____

_____

JUNE

Best Parties and Entertainment

JUNE

My Worst Day

JUNE

My Finest Adventure

JULY

It was a great treat to us to be
turned out into the Home Paddock or the old orchard: the grass was
so cool and soft to our feet; the air was so sweet, and the freedom to
do as we liked – to gallop, lie down, roll over on our backs, or nibble
the sweet grass – was so pleasant. Then, as we stood together under
the shade of the large chestnut-tree, was a very good time for talking.

THOUGHTS FOR
JULY

Today sports camp begins again.
I'm in Cindy's group for the first
week of camp. For competition
week I'm in Mike's group and for
lip-sync we did "I'm to

My Best Day

_____

_____

_____

_____

_____

sexy for my shirt," and
all the boys took off
their shirts.

JULY

Best Parties and Entertainments

JULY

My Worst Day

July

My Finest Adventure

AUGUST

"Let us cheer up and have a run to the other end of the orchard. I believe the wind has blown down some apples, and we may just as well eat them as for the slugs to have them." Merrylegs's suggestions could not be resisted; so we broke off our long conversation and got up our spirits by munching some very sweet apples which lay scattered on the grass.

THOUGHTS FOR
AUGUST

My Best Day

AUGUST

_____

_____

_____

_____

_____

_____

Best Parties and Entertainment

_____

_____

_____

_____

AUGUST

My Worst Day

AUGUST

My Finest Adventure

SEPTEMBER

As for us, our greatest pleasure was when we were saddled for a riding party – the master on Ginger, the mistress on me, and the young ladies on Sir Oliver and Merrylegs. It was so cheerful to be trotting and cantering all together that it always put us in high spirits. I had the best of it, for I always carried the mistress. Her weight was little, her voice sweet, and her hand so light on the rein that I was guided almost without feeling it.

THOUGHTS FOR
SEPTEMBER

My Best Day

September

Best Parties and Entertainment

SEPTEMBER

My Worst Day

September

My Finest Adventure

_____

_____

_____

_____

_____

OCTOBER

When my harness was taken off,
I did not know what I should do first – eat the grass, roll over on my
back, lie down and rest, or have a gallop across the meadow out of
sheer spirits at being free; so I did all by turns.

THOUGHTS FOR
OCTOBER

My Best Day

OCTOBER

Best Parties and Entertainment

OCTOBER

◦◆‑◆◦◦◆‑◦

_____

_____

_____

_____

_____

_____

_____

◦◆‑◆◦◦◆‑◦

My Worst Day

_____

_____

_____

_____

_____

◦◆‑◦◦◆‑◦

OCTOBER

My Finest Adventure

November

The winter came in early with a great deal of cold and wet. There was snow, sleet, or rain almost every day for weeks, changing only to keen driving winds or sharp frosts. We all felt it very much. When it is a dry cold, a couple of good thick rugs will keep the warmth in us; but when it is soaking rain, they soon get wet through and are no good.

THOUGHTS FOR
NOVEMBER

My Best Day

NOVEMBER

Best Parties and Entertainments

NOVEMBER

My Worst Day

NOVEMBER

My Finest Adventure

DECEMBER

Christmas and the New Year are very merry times for some people; but for cabmen and cabmen's horses these times are no holiday, though they may be a harvest. There are so many parties, balls, and places of amusement open that the work is hard and often late. Sometimes driver and horse, shivering with cold, have to wait for hours in the rain and frost, whilst the merry people within are dancing to the music.

THOUGHTS FOR
DECEMBER

My Best Day

DECEMBER

Best Parties and Entertainments

DECEMBER

_____

_____

_____

_____

_____

_____

_____

My Worst Day

_____

_____

_____

_____

DECEMBER

My Finest Adventure

NEW YEAR'S RESOLUTIONS

LAST YEAR'S RESOLUTIONS
I HAVE KEPT

IMPORTANT ADDRESSES AND TELEPHONE NUMBERS